ICELANDIC PONIES

For a free color catalog describing Gareth Stevens' list of high-quality books, call 1-800-542-2595 (USA) or
1-800-461-9120 (Canada). Gareth Stevens' Fax: (414) 225-0377.

Library of Congress Cataloging-in-Publication Data available upon request from publisher.
Fax: (414) 225-0377 for the attention of the Publishing Records Department.

ISBN 0-8368-1370-7

This edition first published in North America in 1995 by
Gareth Stevens Publishing
1555 North RiverCenter Drive, Suite 201
Milwaukee, Wisconsin 53212, USA

First published in Great Britain in 1994 by Sunburst Books, Deacon House, 65 Old Church Street, London, SW3 5BS.
Photographs © 1989 Franckh'sche Verlagshandlung, W. Keller & Co., Stuttgart, Germany. Text © 1994 Sunburst Books.
Additional end matter © 1995 by Gareth Stevens Publishing.
Photograph on page 15 by Elisabeth Kellner.

U.S. Series Editor: Patricia Lantier-Sampon
U.S. Editor: Barbara J. Behm

Printed in Mexico

2 3 4 5 6 7 8 9 9 99 98 97 96

MAGNIFICENT HORSES OF THE WORLD

ICELANDIC PONIES

Photography by
Tomáš Míček

Text by
Dr. Hans-Jörg Schrenk

Gareth Stevens Publishing
MILWAUKEE

Icelandic Ponies are small and quick. They have long heads, bright eyes, and short ears. Their manes and forelocks are thick and long.

In A.D. 874, a group of Viking farmers left their homeland of Norway. They set sail toward the uninhabited island of Iceland, where they planned to make their new home. They left Norway because they did not want to be under the strict rule of King Harald Fairhair.

The ships carried men, women, children, cattle, and horses. The horses were the stocky, Germanic type. The settlers also brought another breed of horse to Iceland from the coasts of Ireland and Scotland. These horses were Celtic in origin. They were lighter and more refined than the Germanic horses. These two groups of horses produced offspring that are now known as Icelandic Ponies. They have been bred for over a thousand years in Iceland. About sixty thousand Icelandic Ponies live in Iceland today.

Iceland is not a tropical paradise for these small horses. The climate is bitterly cold, and the land is barren. To survive, Icelandic Ponies have had to overcome an extremely hostile environment that includes cold temperatures, wind, rain, heavy snow, and ice storms.

This harsh environment, however, is the reason Icelandic Ponies have developed their extraordinary hardiness and undemanding nature. Because of their strength, Icelandic Ponies can be used for every type of heavy work. Yet, they are also important in the world of sports. They are fierce competitors in racing and dressage.

Icelandic Ponies in their element, running wild in the herd through the wind and rain.

The characteristics of Icelandic Ponies vary according to the region of Iceland in which they live. In northern Iceland, near Skagafjördur, the horses have slender limbs, are very docile, and have a smooth gait. Icelandic Ponies in southern Iceland near Hornafjördur are larger and tougher. They lack the smooth gait that makes a good riding horse.

A herd in full gallop. Most Icelandic Ponies live in semi-wild herds in the hard-to-reach highlands and steep valleys of Iceland.

The goal of Icelandic Pony breeders is to produce a robust, peaceful horse with a smooth gait. Performance is more important than appearance.

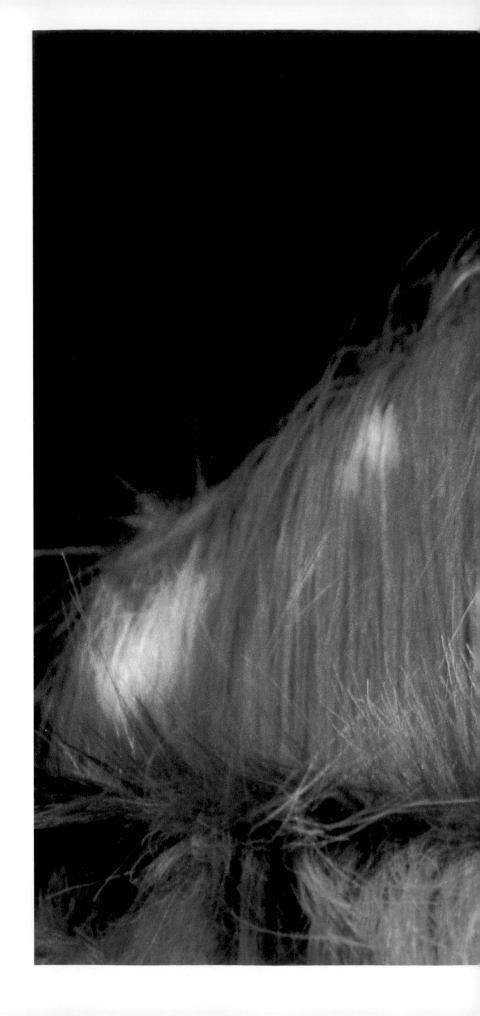

These Icelandic Ponies are from what is known as the Roudblessot Hestar line. They are chestnut in color with white points. Horses from this line have long been known as the best riding horses in Iceland.

Icelandic Ponies give birth to their foals in summer.

12

This foal is only a few days old and is still unsteady on its legs.
It will stay close to its mother until it is better able to
take care of itself.

These two older foals have formed a friendship with one another.

Foals drink mother's milk for about six months.

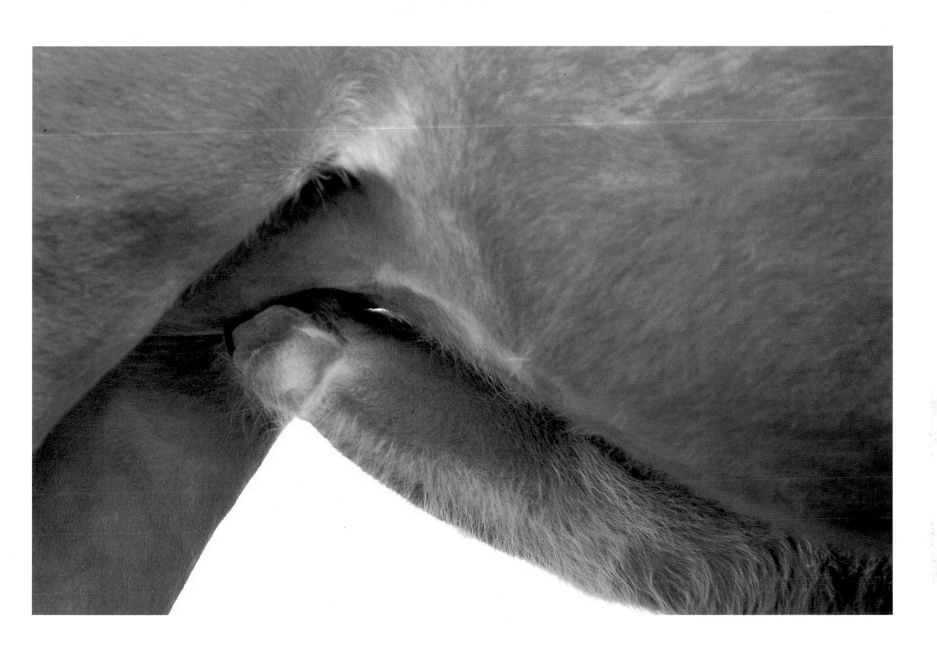

*After about six months, the foals are divided into herds
of colts and fillies.*

This newborn will spend the entire summer grazing alongside its mother in the green meadows.

After reaching six months of age, foals begin to eat grass and herbs.

Geldings gallop through the mountain meadows of summer.

*Within a herd, male horses constantly play-fight. This allows them to
express their strength and challenge what is known as the
hierarchy. This play fighting can become a serious
business for the stallions when they fight for
their ranking in the herd.*

Through gentle nips with his teeth, a colt tries to start a play-fight.

The strongest feature of the Icelandic Pony is its gait. A true Icelandic Pony can walk, trot, canter, and gallop. In addition, it has two other gaits – the tilt and the pace.

The tilt can be compared to the walk. During the walk, the Icelandic Pony always has two or three hooves on the ground. In the tilt, only one or two hooves are on the ground at a time.

During the pace, legs on either side of the horse work together. This is a racing gait. Because this gait is difficult for the horses to keep up, races are limited in length.

As autumn closes in, these Icelandic Ponies already have their thick winter coats. Even though temperatures will soon start to become very low, the horses still prefer the outdoors to a barn.

Icelandic Ponies have a beautiful, silky mane. The mane usually divides in the middle, falling on both sides of the neck.

This young Icelandic Pony rolls on the ground to scratch its back in the places it cannot reach with its teeth or hooves.

The coats of Icelandic Ponies come in different colors. The most common colors are chestnut, bay, black, cream, and gray.

The gelding showing his teeth seems to be the highest-ranking horse in this herd. He is showing his teeth to stop the other horses from overtaking him.

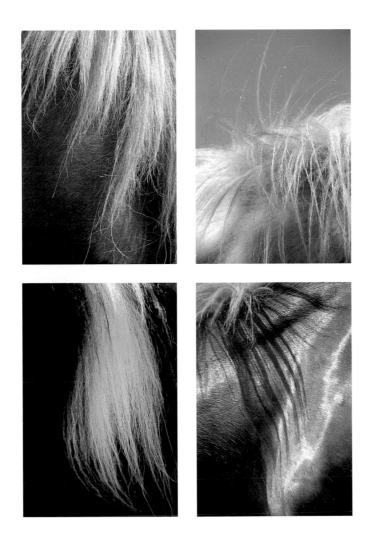

The manes of Icelandic Ponies also come in a variety of colors.

Icelandic Ponies are not comfortable in warm, closed stables. They are used to having freedom. They feel best in the open air and in a herd, which is what they have been used to for hundreds of years.

Ideally, the horses should have access to a shelter, but not be confined to one. They will usually only make use of a shelter when it is raining heavily, when the sun is too hot, or when they are bothered by flies. Their coats are so thick that snow and cold do not bother them.

Even when the weather is cold and damp, Icelandic Ponies prefer to be outside.

A "liver-chestnut" gelding with a white mane.

From spring through autumn, grass is the basic food for Icelandic Ponies. They require special feed, such as hay, only if they are getting an extra vigorous workout.

Icelandic Ponies at breeding farms start getting used to people at about
the age of four years. At that age, they are "broken," or trained,
and perhaps selected for breeding.

Most of these young stallions will become riding horses. Only the very exceptional ones will be chosen for breeding. One of the most famous breeding areas in Iceland is near Skagafjördur.

Before the 1850s, Icelandic Ponies were found only in Iceland. They began to be exported in 1850. At that time, the small, tough Icelandic Ponies were used to pull heavy coal wagons in the depths of the coal mines in England. By 1950, Icelandic Ponies were being exported to Germany. In 1970, an international association called the European Federation of Friends of the Icelandic Pony was formed. This organization now lists over 25,000 Icelandic Ponies living in areas of the world beyond Iceland.

Icelandic Ponies find pleasure in winter. They are sure-footed and frisky in the snow and cold.

Today, Icelandic Ponies have a huge following throughout Europe. Their calm, but tough, personalities make them excellent riding horses. They can easily cover 25-30 miles (40-50 kilometers) a day without problems. They enjoy going on outings in large groups and rarely fight among themselves along the way. Icelandic Ponies are also good competitors in sports activities.

Fast and agile Icelandic Ponies gallop through the snow in the fading light of the winter sun.

Young stallions fight in the snow. Icelandic stallions are famous for their high spirits.

Rearing up on their hind legs is part of the ritual of stallion fights. From this position, a stallion can inflict heavy blows with the forelegs on an opponent's chest.

This young stallion has detected an interesting fragrance in the air and flares his nostrils in response.

GLOSSARY

bay — reddish brown in color.

breed — animals having specific traits; to produce offspring.

canter — a slow, easy gallop.

chestnut — reddish brown in color.

colts — male horses under the age of four years.

fillies — young female horses.

foals — newborn male or female horses.

forelocks — locks of hair growing from the front of the head.

gait — a way of walking or running.

gallop — a fast way of running by an animal, such as a horse.

gelding — a male horse that has had his reproductive organs removed.

herd — a number of animals of one kind that stay together and travel as a group.

hierarchy — the ranking of individuals within a group from most to least powerful.

mane — long hair around the neck of a horse.

pony — a breed of horse that remains small even as an adult.

stallions — mature male horses used for breeding.

trot — a four-legged animal's slow running gait.

MORE BOOKS ABOUT HORSES

Complete Book of Horses and Horsemanship. C. W. Anderson (Macmillan)
The Great Book of Horses. Catherine Dell (R. Rourke)
Guide to the Horses of the World. Caroline Silver (Exeter)
Horse Breeds and Breeding. Jane Kidd (Crescent)
Horse Happy: A Complete Guide to Owning Your Own Horse. Barbara J. Berry (Bobbs-Merrill)
Horses and Riding. George Henschel (Franklin Watts)
The Ultimate Horse Book. Elwyn Hartley Edwards (Dorling Kindersley)
Wild and Wonderful Horses. Cristopher Brown, ed. (Antioch)

VIDEOS

The Art of Riding Series. (Visual Education Productions)
The Horse Family. (International Film Bureau)
Horses! (Encyclopedia Britannica)
The Mare and Foal. (Discovery Trail)
Nature: Wild Horses. (Warner Home Video)

PLACES TO WRITE

Here are some places to write for more information about horses. When you write, include your name and address, and be specific about the information you would like to receive. Don't forget to enclose a stamped, self-addressed envelope for a reply.

National Association for Humane
    and Environmental Education
P.O. Box 362
East Haddam, CT 06423-0362

Horse Council of British Columbia
5746B 176A Street
Cloverdale, British Columbia
V3S 4C7

INDEX